DISCOVERING THE UNITED STATES

Wyoming

BY CHRISTINE LAYTON

Kids Core
An Imprint of Abdo Publishing
abdobooks.com

abdobooks.com

Published by Abdo Publishing, a division of ABDO, PO Box 398166, Minneapolis, Minnesota 55439. Copyright © 2025 by Abdo Consulting Group, Inc. International copyrights reserved in all countries. No part of this book may be reproduced in any form without written permission from the publisher. Kids Core™ is a trademark and logo of Abdo Publishing.

Printed in the United States of America, North Mankato, Minnesota.
052024
092024

Cover Photo: Cody Rarick/Shutterstock Images
Interior Photos: *Time Exposure: The Autobiography of William Henry Jackson*, 4; William H. Jackson/Heritage Art/Heritage Images/Hulton Archive/Getty Images, 4–5; Shutterstock Images, 7, 15, 18, 22, 28 (Old Faithful), 28 (Devils Tower); Brian Lasenby/Shutterstock Images, 8 (top left); Ann Cantelow/Shutterstock Images, 8 (top right); Tom Reichner/Shutterstock Images, 8 (bottom left); O. S. Fisher/Shutterstock Images, 8 (bottom right); Kyle Spradley Photography/Shutterstock Images, 10; Helen H. Richardson/Denver Post/Getty Images, 12–13; William Mancebo/Getty Images Sport/Getty Images, 16; Cheri Alguire/iStockphoto, 20–21; Jessica Rinaldi/Boston Globe/Getty Images, 25; Galyna Andrushko/Shutterstock Images, 26; Red Line Editorial, 28 (map), 29 (top); Alla Gill/Shutterstock Images, 28 (Grand Teton); Sandra Foyt/Shutterstock Images, 29 (bottom)

Editor: Haley Williams
Series Designer: Katharine Hale

Library of Congress Control Number: 2023949376

Publisher's Cataloging-in-Publication Data

Names: Layton, Christine, author.
Title: Wyoming / by Christine Layton
Description: Minneapolis, Minnesota: Abdo Publishing, 2025 | Series: Discovering the United States | Includes online resources and index.
Identifiers: ISBN 9781098294229 (lib. bdg.) | ISBN 9798384913498 (ebook)
Subjects: LCSH: U.S. states--Juvenile literature. | Wyoming--History--Juvenile literature. | Western States (U.S.)--Juvenile literature. | Physical geography--United States--Juvenile literature.
Classification: DDC 973--dc23

All population data taken from:
"Estimates of Population by Sex, Race, and Hispanic Origin: April 1, 2020 to July 1, 2022." *US Census Bureau, Population Division*, June 2023, census.gov.

CONTENTS

CHAPTER 1
The First National Park 4

CHAPTER 2
The People of Wyoming 12

CHAPTER 3
Places in Wyoming 20

State Map 28
Glossary 30
Online Resources 31
Learn More 31
Index 32
About the Author 32

William Henry Jackson, *top*, lived from 1843 to 1942. Many of his photographs, *bottom*, are kept in historic collections today.

The First National Park

It was 1871. Ferdinand Hayden and William Henry Jackson were exploring an area in Wyoming. Hayden was a scientist. He was collecting data on the land. Jackson was a photographer. He took hundreds of pictures of the area.

After several months, Jackson and Hayden went back home with their notes and pictures of Wyoming. Many Americans were amazed by the beautiful photographs. US lawmakers saw Jackson's pictures of **canyons**, hot springs, and forests. They believed the land needed to be protected.

In March 1872, US president Ulysses S. Grant signed a law protecting 2 million acres (809,400 ha) of Wyoming's land. The law created the United States' first national park. The park was called Yellowstone.

Today, Yellowstone is one of the most famous US national parks. Millions of people visit every year. Yellowstone continues to be an important part of Wyoming's history.

Waterfalls flow through Yellowstone National Park.

Land

Wyoming is in the US region called the West. It borders six other states. Montana is to the north. South Dakota and Nebraska are in the east. To the south are Colorado and Utah. And Idaho borders Wyoming in the west.

Wyoming Facts

DATE OF STATEHOOD
July 10, 1890

CAPITAL
Cheyenne

POPULATION
581,381

AREA
97,813 square miles
(253,335 sq km)

STATE BIRD
Western meadowlark

STATE TREE
Plains cottonwood

STATE FLOWER
Indian paintbrush

STATE MAMMAL
Bison

Each US state has a different population, size, and capital city. States also have state symbols.

Wyoming's land is very different across the state. There are forests, deserts, and canyons. The Great **Plains** cover eastern Wyoming. Plants such as shrubs and short grasses grow there. The landscape has many low hills and valleys.

Wyoming also has a lot of mountains. The Rocky Mountains cross most of the western part of the state. The Wyoming **Basin** lies between mountain ranges. There, water flows into rivers that cut between the mountains. Major rivers include the Platte River and Yellowstone River.

Dinosaur Dig

Many **fossils** have been discovered in Wyoming. Scientists found tiny fossils from about 1.7 billion years ago in the Medicine Bow Mountains of southern Wyoming. They also found the bones of many well-known dinosaurs, including *Triceratops* and *Tyrannosaurus rex*.

Pronghorns are one of many types of animals that live in Wyoming's Red Desert.

Much of western Wyoming is covered by desert. The Red Desert has sand dunes and many rock formations. Art from thousands of years ago is carved into the rock walls there.

Climate

The climate in Wyoming is mostly cool, dry, and windy. The mountains can block rain from moving across the state. But in the winter, Wyoming gets a lot of snow. Snow falls in the mountains and melts in the spring. Summers bring warm weather to the plains and basins. But the high mountains stay cool.

Explore Online

Visit the website below. Does it give any new information about the land of Wyoming that wasn't in Chapter One?

Our Wyoming

abdocorelibrary.com/discovering-wyoming

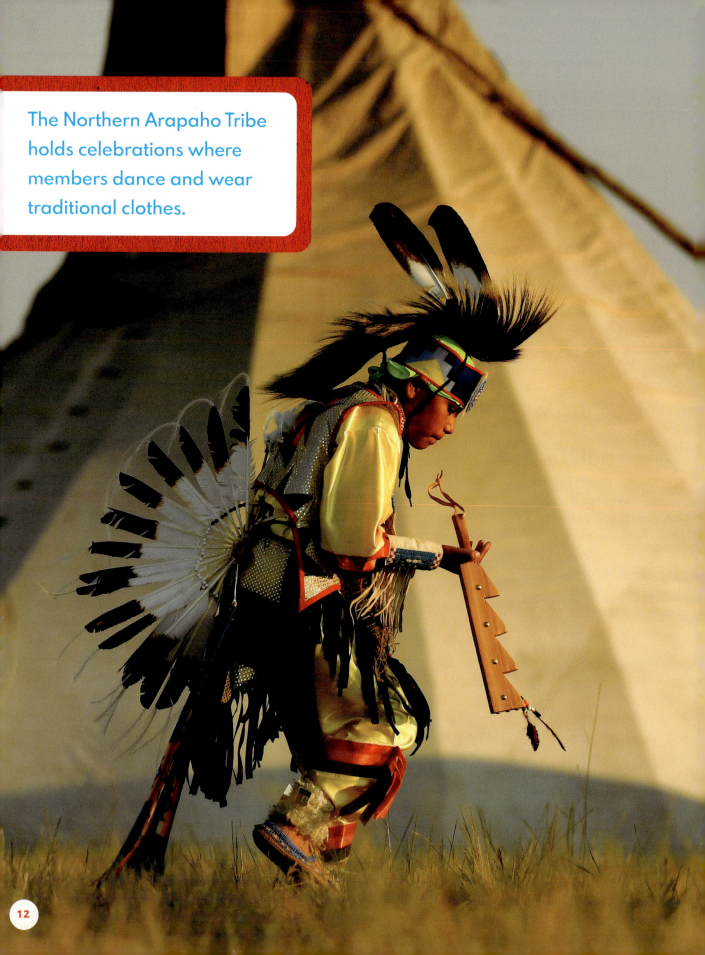

The Northern Arapaho Tribe holds celebrations where members dance and wear traditional clothes.

CHAPTER 2

The People of Wyoming

American Indians have lived in Wyoming for more than 12,000 years. Early people living in Wyoming included groups of tribes known as the Plains Indians. The Plains Indians were **nomadic**. Today, Wyoming has two federally recognized tribes.

They are the Northern Arapaho Tribe and Eastern Shoshone Tribe. Many members live on the Wind River Reservation in central Wyoming.

White European explorers began arriving in Wyoming in the late 1700s. They wanted to catch wild animals and sell their fur. During the mid-1800s, hundreds of thousands of Americans began moving out west. Some settled in Wyoming.

Wyoming has the lowest population of any US state. In 2022, almost 582,000 people lived in the state. White people made up 83 percent of Wyoming's population. About 11 percent of people were Hispanic or Latino. American Indian people made up almost 3 percent of the population. And around 1 percent were Black.

The Wyoming state flag shows a bison and the state's seal.

Culture

Many people in Wyoming celebrate the culture of the American West. Rodeos are very popular in the state. At these events, people ride bulls and throw ropes to catch young cows.

One event at Cheyenne Frontier Days is barrel racing. Contestants ride their horses through a pattern of barrels.

Cowboys started holding rodeos in the 1800s. The world's largest rodeo takes place in Cheyenne during the Frontier Days festival.

People in Wyoming enjoy the outdoors. Camping, hiking, and watching wildlife are popular activities. Many also enjoy skiing and snowboarding in Wyoming's mountains.

Food is another important part of Wyoming's culture. One popular dish is the chuck wagon dinner. It was created by American cowboys. The meal usually has meat or fish such as bison or trout. It also includes baked beans, biscuits, and coffee.

Winter Fun

People come from around the world to visit Wyoming's snowy mountains. The state has many ski resorts. On the mountainsides, people ski, snowboard, and snowshoe. When lakes freeze over in the winter, people drill holes into the ice to go fishing. Some people even swim in natural hot springs in the winter.

Coal is one important resource that people mine in Wyoming.

Industry

Many people in Wyoming have jobs in agriculture. They raise livestock such as cows, pigs, and sheep. Other farmers grow crops, including wheat, oats, barley, and corn.

Mining is another big industry in Wyoming. Many miners drill for oil and **natural gas**. These resources are used to make electricity. Some miners also explore the land for gold and other minerals.

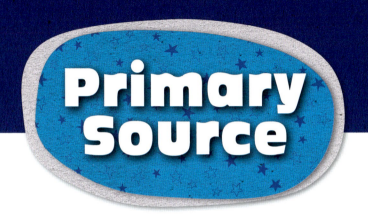

In the 1830s, American Indian chief Arapooish from the Crow Nation talked about traveling to Wyoming's mountains in the summer:

> [You] can draw up under the mountains, where the air is sweet and cool, the grass fresh, and the bright streams come tumbling out of the snow-banks.

Source: Gregory Nickerson. "Before Wyoming." *WyoHistory.org*, 30 July 2019, wyohistory.org. Accessed 28 Sept. 2023.

Comparing Texts

Think about the quote. Does it support the information in this chapter? Or does it give a different perspective? Explain how in a few sentences.

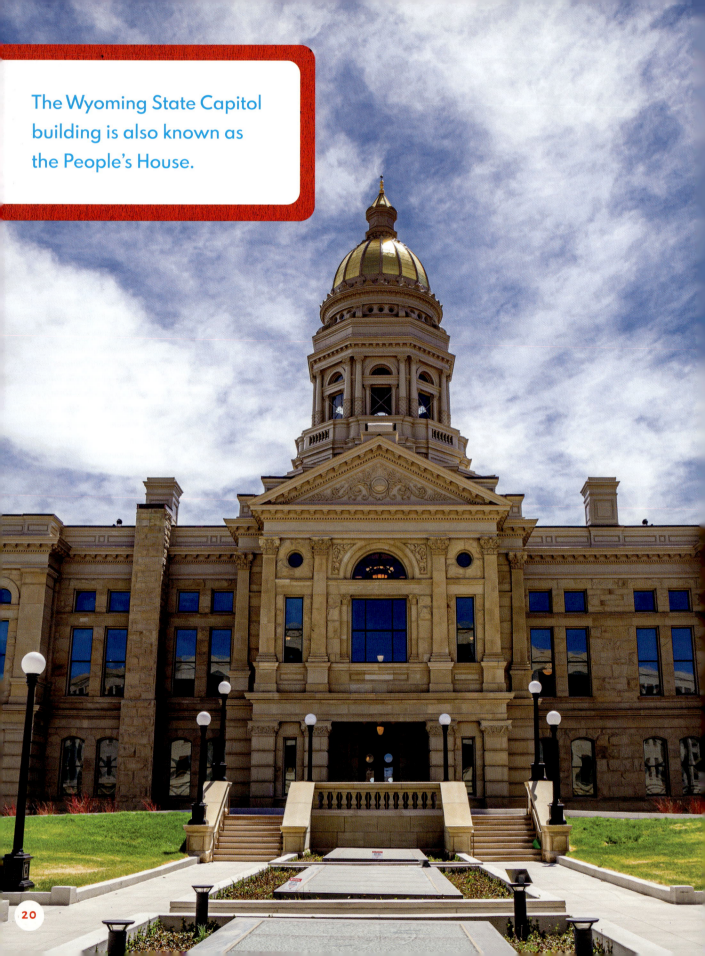

The Wyoming State Capitol building is also known as the People's House.

CHAPTER 3

Places in Wyoming

Wyoming's capital, Cheyenne, is the state's largest city. The next-largest city is Casper. The rest of the state's towns and cities are small and spread far apart. Other big towns in Wyoming include Laramie, Cody, and Jackson.

Grand Prismatic Spring is a hot spring in Yellowstone National Park. Its bright colors come from bacteria living in the water.

National Parks

Wyoming has several national parks. Yellowstone National Park is in the northwestern part of the state. Yellowstone is home to many **geysers**. The Yellowstone River flows through a canyon in the park. Visitors can hike and camp in Yellowstone. They can also see wildlife such as grizzly bears and wolves.

Grand Teton National Park is also in northwestern Wyoming. This park has hiking trails and huge mountains. Animals such as bighorn sheep can be found there.

Old Faithful

Old Faithful is the most famous geyser in the United States. It is one of about 500 geysers found in Yellowstone. Explorers gave Old Faithful its name in 1870. The geyser erupts about 20 times a day. It can shoot water between 100 and 180 feet (30.5–55 m) into the air.

There are also many lodges and resorts people can stay at while visiting the park.

Landmarks

Wyoming has several landmarks. **Fossil** Butte National Monument is in the desert of southwestern Wyoming. Visitors can see the fossils of many kinds of animals in the area's rock formations.

Devils Tower National Monument is found on the prairie in northeastern Wyoming. It is considered an important place to the Plains American Indians. Devils Tower stands 1,267 feet (386 m) above the surrounding land.

Jackson Hole is a valley near Jackson, Wyoming. It is a very popular tourist attraction.

Mountaineers climb Devils Tower using cracks in the rocks. Thousands of people climb the formation every year.

Many people enjoy skiing, snowboarding, and white water rafting there. Flaming Gorge National Recreation Area is in southwestern Wyoming. It is also a popular place to do all kinds of outdoor activities.

The Green River flows through Flaming Gorge National Recreation Area.

Wyoming is home to many natural wonders. People can learn about the state's history and culture. They can also see its beautiful land and wildlife. And those who love the outdoors can ski and hike in the mountains. There are so many things to experience in Wyoming.

Further Evidence

Look at the website below. Does it give any new evidence to support Chapter Three?

Wyoming

abdocorelibrary.com/discovering -wyoming

State Map

KEY
 Capital Park
 City or town Point of interest

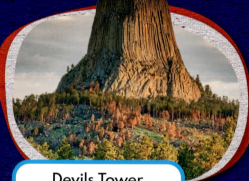
Devils Tower National Monument

Old Faithful

Grand Teton National Park

Wyoming: The Equality State

Fossil Butte National Monument

Glossary

basin
land that dips into Earth's surface, sometimes filled with water

canyon
a deep, narrow valley cut by a river through rock. This process, called erosion, can take thousands or millions of years

fossil
the very old, preserved remains of an animal or plant

geyser
a hot spring that occasionally shoots water into the air

natural gas
a mix of gases found underground that can be used as fuel

nomadic
relating to people who move from place to place

plains
areas of flat, treeless land

Online Resources

To learn more about Wyoming, visit our free resource websites below.

Visit **abdocorelibrary.com** or scan this QR code for free Common Core resources for teachers and students, including vetted activities, multimedia, and booklinks, for deeper subject comprehension.

Visit **abdobooklinks.com** or scan this QR code for free additional online weblinks for further learning. These links are routinely monitored and updated to provide the most current information available.

Learn More

Ard, Cath. *Yellowstone*. Flying Eye Books, 2023.

Perdew, Laura. *Grassland Biomes*. Abdo, 2024.

Tieck, Sarah. *Wyoming*. Abdo, 2020.

Index

Cheyenne, 8, 16, 21
climate, 11
cowboys, 16–17

deserts, 8, 10, 24
Devils Tower National
   Monument, 24

Eastern Shoshone Tribe, 14

Grand Teton National
   Park, 23

Hayden, Ferdinand, 5–6

industries, 18

Jackson, William Henry, 5–6
Jackson Hole, 24–25

mountains, 9, 11, 17, 19, 23, 27

Northern Arapaho Tribe, 14

Plains Indians, 13, 24
population, 8, 14

Yellowstone National Park,
   6, 22–23

About the Author

Colorado children's author Christine Layton loves the wilderness of Wyoming. When Christine isn't traveling and writing books for kids, she enjoys board games, hiking, and puzzles. She also loves to help kids and adults get excited about reading and writing.